INTERNET GIRLFRIEND

```
      00                    10
   00011010101          01000001010
  101010100101010     10100010111010
 0100101010101010101  0101001010101010101
 01010101010101010101 0101010101010100
1010100010101010101010 1010101001010101010
010101010010101010101010101010101010101010
1010101010101000101010000001101010010010
100101010101001010101010101010010101000
10101010101001010101010101010101010100
01010101111101010010101010101001010010
 0101010010101010010100100100010010
  1010100010101001001010001010101010
   01010101010010010101001001001010
    1001010101001010101010100101010
     10010010100010101010100101010
      100100101001010101010101010101
       00100010010101010010101010
        101010100100101010
         100101010100101
          010010101001
           01010101
            0101
```

Stephanie Valente

Praise for Spell Work (Giallo)

Stephanie Valente's *Spell Work* explores the strength within magic's ephemera. With knife-sharp language and bejeweled imagery, Valente reminds us that, at times, desire can be more powerful and delicious than attaining that which is desired. In "/Spell: Enter Fantasy Land /" the poet writes: "1. buy the ticket / 2. enter through the turnstile / 3. visualize yourself with a rose gold crown / 4. exit through the gift shop". To read Valente's masterfully aware, refreshingly acerbic, and gorgeously fantastic poetic grimoire is to feel all the euphoria of magic without any of the sacrifice

— *Kailey Tedesco, author of She Used to be on a Milk Carton, Lizzie, Speak, and FOREVERHAUS*

Stephanie Valente's Spell Work is glamour danger, and fun thought alchemy. Each poem shifts into the next, an invitation to death and more, "enter through the turnstile." A night circuit with a flower bright charge.

— *Monique Quintana, Author of Cenote City (Clash Book, 2019)*

Praise for Internet Girlfriend

Stephanie Valente's *internet girlfriend* oozes with style. In an age of Y2K nostalgia, this collection of poems somehow makes the dial-up days feel glamorous while also experimenting with form in such a way that makes me excited for the future, assuming it will contain more poetry like this. These poems are a mystical time warp, a sequined occult ritual, and a lip gloss kiss stain emoji all at once. Valente writes: "please make / everything feel / opalescent // now and / forever" & that is exactly what every single poem in this collection does.

— Kailey Tedesco, author of *She Used to be on a Milk Carton*, *Lizzie, Speak*, and *FOREVERHAUS*

In Valente's debut book, *Internet Girlfriend,* we go on enchanting dates with poems. They envelop us in a simultaneously glossy and sinister sheen, turning us *on*—maybe even to our meta-reality. As words, glitching pixels, codes, and messaging accumulate, we peer into the sheer magic of a loose language, a reckoning with our inner teenager, and wherein the internet as our lover; Meaning develops past the screens. We become engaged to our witch hood.

—Katherine Factor, author of *A Sybil Society,* winner of the *Interim* Test Site Poetry prize

Stephanie Valente's *Internet Girlfriend* serves up a vivid nostalgia for a time when the newness of the internet intersected with the newness of sexuality for a generation of teen girls; those who dealt with the impossibility of their cultural irrelevance with ouija boards, witchcraft and fantasy, and eventually, and finally, by embracing a form of empowerment in the many variations of sexual attention their youth afforded them. The reader travels back to the days when we would consult the magic 8-ball "if i could love/ myself,/ it says:/ keep dreaming/ keep dreaming" but is also granted several visions of the future. "Here is how our great romance ends" begins one of my favorite of these poems, "oracle" which shows battle scars, but also wisdom; and in "palmistry" the speaker predicts, among other things, how despite or maybe because of these numerous difficult experiences "in the future, you'll learn to love yourself and it feels strange".

—Carrie Nassif, author of *Lithopaedion* (Finishing Line Press)

To Tom, the best internet connection, and to gURLpages, America Online, and Live Journal.

a/s/l?

interests: easy makeouts, plastic light,

electroplated glass,

fortune-telling fish, 3-megapixel portraits,

lust like most people,

the internet is a personality test,

prisms,

decide who you really are, or just unicorns

tell me more about enlightenment,

you make me feel like *the little prince*.

i enjoy mathematics, but the solution

should be has too many variables, and the result

seashells

all the way

here.

your thumb across my lip feels erotic,

if i knew what it felt like in real life,

flip phones were the most perfect phones

in history,

i don't understand why, but

our love story would have subtitles.

ballad of sporty spice

the best girls wear tracksuits and i didn't
always think so, thought i had to be
red and blonde streaked sultry smeared
eyeshadow looking to belong in
places i didn't belong in when i grew
up, turns out, i was pure
slicked back ponytail, a velvet two piece,
feeling powerful in not giving a damn.

relax kristy, it's just the dark lord

that spring, i decided to become a witch
control the weather, adjust term paper deadlines,
a new *wet seal* outfit, the plaid number, with straps
maybe, maaaaybe, maybe, kiss my crush

i didn't see the harm, you know
it's not turning the universe upside its head
i wasn't even asking for a bigger hourly rate

i said to kristy, let's have a good summer
let's make it interesting, let's make it a little

sinister

we all needed to relax, i kept a little piece
of quartz, like a darling piece of ivory
tucked in my denim shorts,

for luck, for power, i said my prayers at night
i crafted twigs into pentagrams,

my lips looked a little darker, just rogue,

just full of blood

it was all in the name of good fortune,
and yeah, a prom date that felt mystical all over
i just wanted my eyes to sparkle, and smell
like that expensive coconut lotion, forever,
like running with unicorns

at the next circle meeting, she struck me down.

california diary

–after *Amalia's Diary*

even now, i think about it
secret charms, a real portal
full of handwriting
private spells that no one knows
except me, tucked away
reading someone else's
hopes and dreams, a stranger's
fears, but they're real and they're mine
sneaking out to see a man, surrounded in blue
like petals shedding from my hair
like a nightmare, with blue
flowers, and LA dark magic,
too much coca-cola, dark denim,
a car, a hand hitting you, *connecting*
across the face, a future prediction:
purple bruise on cheek bone + brow bone
howling under wolf stars
and reading a girl's diary
again and again and again:
she writes just to me: *it happened to me too*
me too, me too, me too, me too.

teen witch

in reality, i'm just the mortal
sidekick side chick

look at me
like a mirror
like i'm someone
worth a damn

i want a taste of power
i'll drink it like an elixir

stitching white light
around me, writhing

a snake, devouring
the last of its prey.

adventures at the makeout club

[+] milkshake thursday special
[+] new wave is dead
[+] skateboarding all day
[+] eyeshadow sleep red lip nap
[+] give me a record to sing
[+] doing nothing of the sort
[+] i tell lies to cassette tapes
[+] yes, i do like beautiful voices
[+] is there a cure? is this just a confession?
[+] i'm an august baby with a pisces heart
[+] i don't have any photos to share
[+] ten minutes but feels like three hours
[+] cam girl porn with a plot
[+] yellow is an underrated color
[+] i'm certain we have nothing in common

baby's first tarot cards

untapped power feels like a drug.
i wish i was an oracle, magnificent,
gazing into prisms, swirling visions
in a constellation of stars,
page-turning answers, god, imagine
imagine that power, everyone,
everyone would kiss me at parties,
especially at the end of the night,
they'll love me and love me and love me
like ice-cold pepsi after a run, like a shiny gem
they'll love me more than TV, the internet,
the witch girl that can see the future
can you suffocate from kissing?
too much, a glorious way to die—
lay the cards out, tell me the answers.

you vs. the girl they told you not to worry about

is she pretty?
what is her hair like?
does she know how to smile?

does she have small hands?
do ghosts visit her in dreams, too?
does she wake up just to fall back asleep?
are there people who listen to her voice?

will you let me love you?
probably not, but there's no harm
in practicing. i hear computers do it best.

the universe said be anything, so i became
a babysitter

life could be summed up as
a series of phantom phone calls, measured
with curious charges,

        psychic twins
        too many phone calls
        w/ boys

strikes, summer ten dollars bills
folded up three extra times in my pocket
only to find again, in someone else's living room
and not enough orange soda

i am the babysitter,
forgetting a list of rules, developing
a big crush on someone handsome,
cookies after school,

        homework on the weekends–

braiding my hair, regaling tiny hands
with camp stories, but no ghosts,

        and one story, one missed ghost
        a hot august photograph, kept
        just for myself,

        a treat, in puka shells,
        and hope:

a big sleepover, and a crush
on a girl with glass-blonde hair,
made my cheeks peach-hot,

        we never kissed
        but boy,
        i wanted to.

blue_nails_cam.jpg

more than anything
is a glitter-ice-blue
my nails for the
freshly injected
kardashian,
to men,
15 became
i lied about
my house, my books,
fantasizing,

living in the phantasm
manicure, painting
camera, relaxed hand muscles
lips, pouting like a better
in chat rooms, i used to lie
about my age, always older
21 or 23, then 26 and 27,
my name, my hair, my interests
anything at all worth
in a liquid pool of blue.

cult classic

when we were serpents,
we became witches:

in the summer
a rite of passage began
with britney spears' *heaven on earth*

whispered sacred words,
we transformed to statues
followed by sticky crystals initiations:

> black hair dye left over in the sink
> no ceremonial wine
> pink lady apple lemon seltzer
> our toes chipped in brown lacquer
> your fingers ink-smeared with sigils
> my lips painted horror movie queen red ♛

we were something,

we burned.

first crush

once upon a time, i was bored on the internet. so i fell in love with someone.

a signature conjured green text and angelfire. we started a webring to take over the internet. we had angst, but more importantly, we had glowing text and curiosity.

the 56k dial up noise was a pleasure and a torture. i never held my breath so hard at a dial tone since then.

my buddylist was the wall between us. someone was always there.

what does your voice sound like?
i don't even know what you look like, but i know you are beautiful.
you entice me.
you are enchanting.
what do you do every day?

i fell in love with a computer monitor. it was like sneaking out at night, but i'm just in the living room. wondering who you are and if you like to drink coffee.

in this world, i was always older. i was lying, but in this world everyone lied. you wouldn't even be mad at me if or when you found out the truth. truth was a construct.

can you sneak out?

i already snuck out here with you.

my heart only lived after school and until 3 am. i tell everyone i have long hair to my waist. i tell someone that my lips are naturally strawberry-colored and full and i write poetry that no one reads except the internet.

i'm a virgin.
i like to read books. vampires are my favorite.
what is sex like? tell me everything.

hi, hello. 15/f/here. i want you to love me.

internet girlfriend

two seasons of *sabrina,*
the teenage witch
under my belt
i'm feeling powerful

i sign on AIM after 9pm
dial up noises are wands
just a secret crush

it's always nice,
talking to you, warm rushes
like waves, my heart flutters

you live in
cold cobblestone
unionized
universe
i am a suburb
a cat in a tree

the world feels like it's ending
it's beautiful, i don't want it to stop

this is how i feel: endless
you :), and me :)

i keep your instant messages
like sacred charms,

i reread IMs in the dark
in truth,
your messages
are spells
cast on me

what if
i ran away
to you?
missing forever

i read your texts,
spellbound
some witch
i am.

wish upon a magic 8-ball

there is a secret universe
inside a black ball

a dice of fortunes
i use it to wish
under everything

i tell it
my dreams
my secrets
my lust

i wish on everything[1]
dreams are wishes
wishes are dreams

like glass
floating in night

i ask the ball
if i could love
myself,

it says:
keep dreaming
keep dreaming
keep dreaming
keep dreaming
keep dreaming
keep dreaming.

---

[1] silver coin, stars, numbers, days, rainbows, stones, hope

transcript

–stephanie is available.

me: ~~what does it mean to be human and female?~~
me: ~~how do we find identity or connection?~~
me: ~~why do i always want to buy things?~~
me:
you:

me: hello
you: hi

me: ~~i like you~~
you:

–pleasantries exchanged. time passes.
–white space remains.

you: anyway, i made this mixtape, for
me: :) :) :)
me: ~~i think i am attracted to you~~
me: ~~i like men and women and boys and girls~~
me: ~~and it's a overwhelming~~
me: ~~but i think i like you~~

you: sorry pressed enter too soon lol
you: for a girl i like

–a door open notification sounds.

me: ~~is it me?~~
me: ~~a thousand times yes~~
me: ~~you're my first crush~~
me: sure
me: i'll give it a listen.

–aim freezes.
<connection disrupted>

valentine's day email

```
........@*@*
....@*...we..@* ..............................@*
..@*...could......@* ...................@*...be...@*
.@*...angels.......@*..........@*...burning.......@*
@*...webcams........@*...@*....watching........@*
@*...being watching......*......something.........@*
.@*...dreamy,............or......sacred............@*
..@*..............wouldn't that.................@*
....@*............make us ...................@*
........@*.........something............@*
...........@*............?..............@*
................@*..............@*
...................@*......@*
.....................*..@*
......................@
......................*
......................@
......................*
```

you'll never be patty mayonnaise

imitation is the sincerest form of flattery
say it three times fast and it'll become
true, you'll shed your skin and be a changeling
like magic, so true as vanilla bean lip balm,
a new cruiser bike, fresh cut denim jorts
all you have is truth: sunscreen works,
clocks are right twice a day, the world turns,
time is a construct, and you'll never be the
curly-haired enigma that stole the sweater
vest's heart.

away message

of all the bears in this forest,
you are the most beautiful
i'll let you tear me
apart and tender meat love
is society's best myth, just let
me drown in it — floating, release
i'll remember it all, just like your
rough hands on these jeans, fleeting
like the forest billowing through me.

enter the chat

this is a different kind of tower,
in a different kind of fairy tale:

call boys & hang up on them
laugh with a girl with long curly hair
in your italian class, but tell no one,

don't tell her you want to play
with her hair, ever

the world is already complex,
but the internet is great
a little cove filled with gems

purple, red, orange, and blue too
a place for lovers, and dreamers

we let down our hair: open with dreams
it was glorious, all the laughing

typing, calling, laughing
the world felt so large & so small
all at once

with britney on tv, we were excited
about everything, like browsing rows
of endless pies, so delicious,

all of that sugar rots, but still,
so delicious,

is pop culture a spell or a bad omen?

clear lip gloss

i learned about a dancing plague,
overcome like an aphrodisiac, my lips

so sticky with clear goo, like alien sex
like too much cocaine on a tuesday night.

dancing like there was never yesterday.
dancing because tomorrow is a construct.

i think about covering you in
my clear lip gloss until you can't breathe.

imagine dancing yourself to death. imagine that.

landline

what if voices are spells? it's the 2000s and i
curl myself around a phone every time you call
throaty whims are crystals and pauses dripping in gems
my stones, i hope they shine just as bright,
my voice is long in wings, or the dawn waiting for night sky
i don't have time for texts, only us speaking as if it'll all end
at a moment's notice, so just oil my wings for now.

unfortunately, my rising sign is always right.
change is coming and i have no desire to be prepared.

unicorn

#i look better than my photos and i'm not spending
##a dime
###you're both hungry
####starving
#####you love me, they love me
######daddy after hours, that's what i call
#######your girlfriend
########i am tits in a dress, no bra
#########i'm afraid nothing will ever be as interesting again i am
##########extra tequila sips
###########i am something i am not i am not sure what i am
############i am gilded, rare, and horned
#############i am iridescent fur
##############i'm hotter than you wife; i'm no one's wife
###############i smoked three cigarettes on the walk over here
################to feel something; it burned; i lost my patience
#################the curtain parts, the veil is already thinning
##################this won't last forever i'm already forgetting
###################you're inside me she's on top of me i don't come
##################we cast a black magic spell
#################there's cloves, wine, not enough water
################do you think the spell will come true? could i love you?
###############there's a goblin in my throat; it burns
############i'm not a kind person but you both think so
###########can you love me? probably maybe
##########i'm the star of the show, too worried about reviews
#########love me like a hex, i'll eat your heart maybe
########no one ever made me a mixtape; i'm still raw about it
#######that's the truth really could you make me a tape the way
######he looks at you; he'll look at me; i'll steal him to love him
#####i'll still fuck you but i want to hurt someone's heart
####it's callous it's cruel it's real life that nothing is pretty
###even me sitting here a dress half on spilling over my shoulder
##it's hot, masturbation-worthy how i look nonchalant, how i care too much
#say hello sometime, i promise it will be fun

blue rosaries

boyfriend
girlfriend
kisses
tattoos
bay leaves
death/rebirth
after life
orange oil on
ghost skin
we dreamed
of horses
we were
patron saints
we were
prayers
painted
dark blue
we became
secrets.

setting: you're the star of someone else's horror movie and it's the sequel.

✦ scroll insta until my wrists hurt
✦ i'll wear acrylic tips until i'm dead and then some
✦ paint my hair in liquid opals and nightly moons
✦ i'll fuck you on an altar like it's a rite for the dark lord
✦ i deserve this because
✦ i cast a love spell and never closed the circle
✦ my trauma has a copay
✦ disassociating means i spend 7 hours a day on google
✦ double tap my photos if you like me
✦ free britney spears, because i too scream behind my selfie eyes
✦ there is always more glitter, suffocating us and the entire town
✦ when i die, lay my body on branches and set me on fire

profile pic

call me agent introvert. so, you want me to fill up a text box with information about myself? no, thank you. are you a horse girl or a hearse girl? can you sing like the sun is a dying star? or, is that just an anxiety attack?

† † †

my favorite activity is movie nights. can you fall in love with a girl in a novelty graphic tee like her? do we have the same definition of love or do you have mirror dreams? do crystals still grow in your belly? mine stopped. do you think i'm a darling? someone needs to speak my language.

† † †

it's much too late to do this right now.

† † †

when i grow up, i'll be a neon mother mary on broadband. what does it take, bunny? the moon ran out of arrows to guard the stars. don't threaten me with a good time. that's a useless fact.

erykah1111

the only girl who stuck up for me in the 5th grade is dead. i'm older
now than she'll ever be and getting older still. i wonder who she
would be now or what bands she would be into. she had an ability
to see cool things before they were cool. she had the coolest screen
names. i remember trying to instant message her in high school but
i was too scared she'd never really want to be my friend. i think as
adults we could've really been friends. i think we would've laughed
at some shit and some mixtapes we made. adult me wouldn't have
been so chicken shit. wanting to be friends with her was like wanting
to wear a leather jacket but always putting it back in the closet. i think
she liked alternative and the pixies and le tigre and obscure music
too. i was always more of a garbage fan. i'm sad i never got to say
thank you. thank you.

when driving past a cemetery, hold your breath

i read about it on reddit, and truthfully i look better
in the light of a pixelated webcam like a saint halo headband.

i'm a dead person today, brown hair turned red
sign on to chat, put me in the center of your cyber fantasies

i'm a good slut, i'm the best slut. shiny in holy oil.
love me like you own me. in a collar.

if you don't hold your breath, you'll die tomorrow.
longing is a kind of divinity.

lara croft is my personal icon

first of all,
she doesn't need men
or even women

there is no kissing
only lurking
climbing
running
sighing

solo boat rides
in venice
discovering
icons in tombs
and mountains too

training in a
countryside house
away
from the butler

kill the predators
all on your own
fix a jeep

she has big tits
that are hers alone

i want big tits
and to find

the secret room
to admire
all of my treasures
alone.

astromancy

what if i decided to cast
spells naked?

what if i really did kiss
any fool i wanted to?

stars whisper
thrill me, *touch me*,

the blood of forever
washes over my nakedness.

wouldn't that really be
something?

don't ask me what i'm thinking

you don't want to know, and i'm lost
in a fantasy not about you.

1-800-your-loss

pain is a construct
of reality
like moss
or a hummingbird

it is glass and glowy
it is what it is

we're here
to take it
like a pill
or a communion wafer

you are
church wine
pleasant and
unpleasant

let every piece
of pain be a
legend,

all heroes start
out somewhere,

i'll masturbate
when you leave.

```
*o*o*o*o*o*o*o*o*o*o*o*o*o*o*o*o*o*o*o*o*o*o*
*o*o*o*o*o*o*o*o*o*o*o*o*o*o*o*o*o*o*o*o*o*o*
*o*o*o*o*o*o*o*o*o*o*o*o*o*o*o*o*o*o*o*o*o*o*
*o*o*o*o*o*o*o*o*o*o*o*o*o*o*o*o*o*o*o*o*o*o*
*o*o*o*o*o*THE PLAN IS SIMPLE:o*o*o*o
*o*o*o*o*o*oCELESTIAL LIFE*o*o*o*o*o*
*o*o*o*o*o*oKISSES ON*o*o*o*o*o*o*o*o
*o*o*o*o*o*oMY NECK*o*o*o*o*o*o*o*o*o
*o*o*o*o*o*oSOUR*o*o*o*o*o*o*o*o*o*o*
*o*o*o*o*o*oHOLY WATER*o*o*o*o*o*o*o*
*o*o*o*o*o*oDECISIONS CAST*o*o*o*o*o*
*o*o*o*o*o*oIN AMBERo*o*o*o*o*o*o*o*o
*o*o*o*o*o*oCALCIFYING*o*o*o*o*o*o*o*
*o*o*o*o*o*oCENTURIES*o*o*o*o*o*o*o*o
*o*o*o*o*o*oYOUR TEETH*o*o*o*o*o*o*o*
*o*o*o*o*o*oAREN'T*o*o*o*o*o*o*o*o*o*
*o*o*o*o*o*oTHAT*o*o*o*o*o*o*o*o*o*o*
*o*o*o*o*o*oSHARP¬*o*o*o*o*o*o*o*o*o*
*o*o*o*o*o*oBURN US*o*o*o*o*o*o*o*o*o
*o*o*o*o*o*oUNDER*o*o*o*o*o*o*o*o*o*o
*o*o*o*o*o*oTHE MOON.*o*o*o*o*o*o*o*o
*o*o*o*o*o*o*o*o*o*o*o*o*o*o*o*o*o*o*o
*o*o*o*o*o*o*o*o*o*o*o*o*o*o*o*o*o*o*o
*o*o*o*o*o*o*o*o*o*o*o*o*o*o*o*o*o*o*o
*o*o*o*o*o*o*o*o*o*o*o*o*o*o*o*o*o*o*o
```

do you want to sleep with me? i want to
sleep with you

for $2.99 a minute, i could
think about really being someone

the instant message blinks
i'll get a hotel room and bring whiskey

my lips form a perfect circle
you're 18, right?

my reply is about a surfing scar
two years in misguided teenage antics

you are a buzzcut, small
teeth nipping on plastic straws

blue light face, i smirk
did you watch my cam?

i'll arrive in wobbly lipstick,
i'll leave in a pile of sweat

you are a boy and a girl and i
want to feel in love with somebody

after i go to astrology.com
looking at saturday's past forecast to
press my lips to the screen.

bimbo makeup

holographic
glitter
black
lipstick
silver
transparent
nail polish
babysoft
perfume
dashed with
hope
more
body
glitter
glitter
hairspray
too
lip gloss
that tastes
like
fake
fruit
mix
with
sugar-free
sprite
on my
tongue.

weekend horoscope

i want to fall in love with you—after all, i am a leo
i'll still keep you a dirty secret,
i promise to circle my horoscope
in a magazine in green, a quiz that will connect
your chest to me, the answers are mostly Bs,
i think i love you
i think i don't know what to say
somewhere in-between oversharing
instagrams & letting the blueberries stain my hands
before the photo snaps
& i'll let you coat the fruit all over my tongue
do you understand this feeling? tell me,
call me sweetheart. are you listening?

pink plastic caboodle

i never went to horse camp, or drowned
in coconut-vanilla glitter body spray

i always wanted to sell my soul
for a friendship bracelet

say an oath under the moon,
pale + lovely, cut my palm,

spill blood,
what's mine is yours:

strawberry lip balm,
our favorite horse,

was possessed,
our favorite horse was lucky
our favorite horse cried blood

crushes, sunscreen sack races,
bad cafeteria pizza
meant falling in lust,
scamming

potential lovers, pentagram scars
best friends forever.

you'd think i was a witch or somethin'

sure, why not? let's spell-dabble tonight.
there's a crescent moon on my arm
there's lust in my ribs
there's curiosity in our throats—

there worst thing that will happen
besides broken glass, of course,
is i'll just get you to love me and love me
more than your favorite dessert
maybe it shouldn't happen,
like a surprise smile from a stranger,
leaving you confused on the sidewalk

on a forgettable afternoon.

if you're facing an unplanned pregnancy, furiously google reversal of luck spells.
if you're falling out of sorts with your lover, furiously google love spells.

i have straddled both places, they both feel like loneliness.

isolation is the constant: liquor-shaped coping rituals, a stray cigarette, a call to lucifer.

my strengths are good music to listen to and sending links to my favorite songs.
i coded a magical 8-ball on my homepage, the predictions were right every time.

outside of a bar, i told a beautiful stranger my name was someone else's.

i learned to love a lie in the moment, so i stayed up all night googling power spells.

if you're trying to be opalescent, conjure the ancestors in your instagram.

if you're trying to stay alive, dance under a blue moon or a blood moon like the internet says.

my prayers and spells might seem like casual vulnerability, like cruising under black sky.

i never asked for help with eating disorders, but i'll let a stranger know all about them.

is my vulnerability a blessing or a curse? i'll steal a sliver of time and tell you about it.

the real lede is: there's so much more i could tell you. but, i won't.

god bless america online

away message: time is a construct
away message: taking a disco nap
away message: i'm thinking of you
away message: i'm babysitting
away message: what if...
away message: you put your hand up
away message: ~~my shirt~~ a mirror
away message: i bleed colors
away message: i worry...
away message: i am the queen of ♠
away message: cast a seance
away message: who talks back?
away message: magic 8-balls move themselves
away message: dream parties are overrated
away message: everything is 🐴
away message: i love you
away message: --{--@

the net

like the movie, i want to be sandra bullock
i also want to be me

years and years ahead
find yourself in a relationship that hurts you
you're sensitive to waves, staring at a void
waiting to be pulled under currents

with so many different people in the world
          so many destinies
          venus is in the wrong house
          like a computer virus

unique nightly sky
curse a moon ruled by *romeo + juliet*

my little death is a celestial temple
          scientific nature disputed over our love
          it's just perfume and rosaries, prayer idols
          which control our precious guidebook for life

my natal chart is cold cash, holy mother saint,
reflect my darkest nature, palming bills from a nightstand

reading your email is a carnal desire,
          i still play with my tamagotchi mindlessly
          disassociating is sexier than sex sometimes
          or all the time, i wrap choker necklaces too tightly
          sweetly, my pussy encompasses various concepts.

i am a duality, a circle
that always needs more money in the bank

what awaits us in the future?
you will see why in a minute.

daydreaming

is a lost art which
i perfected over the years.

cosmic sweethearts

i only dream in neon and pink rhinestones
i dye my hair chocolate lilac, to feel
something besides being an earthling,

come to my house, all marble white
shag carpets to confess your daydreams
valley of the dolls meets valley of pretty sins
i pray to transform into shirley manson

there's shadows underneath these colors,
if you look hard enough, if you listen hard enough
lover, i know we're intertwined like blood and wine
i know your name is stitched in stones and gold

my palms drip holy water like rain, catching
each drop like sacred oil, or youth dew, we'll
stay enchanted in laughs, in a tiny moment for part of forever

your laugh is grey and blue and white, but
your dreams are opals and mother of pearls

don't fly too hard, keep my bird of paradise grounded.

ouija board

i never used one, but i'll jump at the chance
to touch your hands, spin a planchette and ask:

> *d-o-y-o-u-w-a-n-t-m-e-?*
>
> > *yes*
> >
> > *-or-*
> >
> > *no*

my lips feel awkward like i should keep talking. but i don't.
we feel for a world through the veil.
is there a rabbit's foot?
a missing tooth?
a crying bride with a bouquet of blue roses?
teen lovers with missing kidneys and hearts?
what's the story? who will tell it for the next hundred years?

it could be anyone. i hope someone calls.
i'll answer, i worry you won't. you don't.
my memory is hazy in this game. arrows shot through my palms.
i remember love and death. birth. laughing. i remember kitchens.
i remember pouring you a drink. i remember bloody noses.
i remember apologizing. i don't remember after.

you can touch me like the world is ending. everything fades.
tell me yes or no. as the wallpaper peels. you stand in a living room.
i'm yelling. you're yelling *love*, and we're drowning. or, we're
 discovering.
i'm not sure. i'll still kiss you like currency. is it death? is it
antidepressants?
is it an anxiety attack by proxy? move your fingers. the caller is
static.
i'm scared to know:

> > > *what if we're*
> > > *the ghosts?*

night time ice cream

it's summertime and we're gods. i'm still uncertain in white sneakers and cherry-colored lip gloss. it almost tastes like soda. do you want a kiss?

put a scoop in a cup, smile at a customer. we are one cigarette break away,
from insanity. it feels like lust. it feels like a private party.
we'll be searching for this feeling for the rest of our lives.

who wants to live that long? i do. i don't. we're all on borrowed time.
time was invented by someone who is dead. what an asshole.

i want you to give me a ride home, but i'm afraid to ask. you ask instead.
plastic spoons, extra soda, top 40s tunes. for once, i look hot in fluorescent light.

you finger the patches on my denim shorts. tell me how good i smell.
like magic. like home. like summer. like typical fake coconuts and sunscreen.
tell me i'm sex and night lights and fuzzy car seats. i'm good hair days

and *oh nice legs, girl* kind of talk. i know you think it. i know you think our noses will bleed. you smile. you say nothing. you put mint chip in a cone.

it's okay, gods don't talk that much.

`same_animal.jpg`

i love sharing a cigarette with you,
not because i like smoking,
because we talk as if we have any kind of authority
the reality is: we know nothing, we're hungry
i'm ravenous, and i know things with you
i always feel weird when i meet someone with my surname
like we're the same panting starving animal

are our teeth the same?
a little yellow near the gums?
do we like the same diamonds?
a little champagne in the middle?
have you pushed so hard on a swing you swore you'd fly off?

i'd like to smoke with you
we'll meet like rabbits but we'll want to be wolves
everyone wants to be a wolf,
but let's compare teeth and noise and i'll ask if you're hungry
chatter through the noise tonight, stay feral, stay starving.

pick-up line

i started reading tarot cards because i wanted to know exactly when
i would have sex.

fetlife

my skin is a little sticky because it's july and i'm wearing a dress that makes my tits look hot. on the subway ride to his reasonably priced one bedroom in little italy, i refer to myself as goth girlfriend, goth gf, goth paramour. i meet you in his shoebox apartment that i would kill to own because it's a good location and little italy makes me think of my ancestors.

we are both his girlfriend and not his girlfriend. we are his un-girlfriend. we are both his girlfriend and not his girlfriend. we are his un-girlfriend.

maybe it's the essential oil perfume. it feels like dancing. it's probably the adrenaline of a threesome between comfortable strangers.

we have $40 to spend on an trendy matcha bar. i buy us two iced matcha lattes and keep the rest. i like to think of it as my service fee. i don't need the money, but i need the money. i need money like sacred kisses all up in my mouth. like a manic episode. i forget about money and being a girlfriend when i take a sip and stare at your tits that look like my tits. i don't care if he gets off but i want to get you off like orchid oil and flowers hidden in my purse.

i feel immortal for no reason. let's make it last as long as possible.

portrait as a vsco girl
—after Rolling Stones, Britney Spears, and the Velvet Underground

the world is burning
i am oceans and beaches and salt

i am perfect lover spells
i am crystals and higher selves
i am your manifest destiny

money is no object
money is everything

i am honey blonde
quick smirks, bedroom smize

i am a long caption on
a panic attack in the bathroom stall

i am naked skin, freckles
i am hidden universes
full of scratchy filtered secrets

i am unknowing
i am knowing

i am: *you can't always get what you want*
i am: *gimme more*

i am young, or
a silver fox,
always beautiful

i'll be your mirror:
whoever you want me to be.

desktop diary

let me be your bimbo,
        a sweet fetish doll
        still has wants and needs.

        in my dream,
        i pass through a doorway

i'm working an old job that i hate
        somehow i'm not on the payroll

        i want freedom
        i want its killjoy sex on me
        i want, i want

falling in love feels like pornography,
        finding out you're a hit on pornhub
        porno lips, porn legs, porno nails

i want it all in glitter and then some

i have sex with you, or someone else
        to feel different, a new kind of holy
            something profane, something
            lana would sing about in private

what is beauty? i ask.
        i'm not expecting you to know
        you're all knowing like a spectral

rub me in gems and jewels and cheap champagne
        the airbnb is always in my name
        holy, sacred slut pining for dick
        showering it off is the best part

my lips turn purple swollen like a singer
so tired of performing.

chlorophyll, ripped petals
tell me i have a different name
i'll answer to nothing, daddy

i text you, but delete it all before hitting send.

swan avatar

is it strange
that i daydream of you?
is it odd
that i wish
to call you mine
& not mine?
not weird, maybe
just longing,
it is the kind of
feeling stained in
an oracle's
hope & fear
i'd love you more
if only you had wings,
who cares if
it's real?
the fantasy is
always better.

myth.txt

file>open>new
nettle stalks, my hair wraps like sparrows
you are my icarus but in the moon
cosmos swirl in your ears, forget about your lungs
or, the ocean rich with sea glass
save>save as>save
tonight, we're thinking of closing the door
the air will still be there, my cosmos swirling at your feet
don't be scared, it's just stars and spells
there's a glitch, but we're still planning
to attend the party. you knock first.
save>save>save

psychic outlaw

i always had the sight.
dream premonitions. sinking throat sucking lumps.
always picked the right tarot cards. shook an 8-ball only once.
better not tell you now. sooner or later, the answer says yes.
i didn't have to wonder what it would be like to be a girl.
named summer. i knew. being alive was enough,
to feel the story. my horoscopes downloaded to my dreams,
faster than phone wire or texts, always bite-sized chunks.
like magic cards without the manna. i always had the sight.
when my most prized possession: glue-on rhinestones,
purple eyeshadow, fraying puka shell necklace from a
willowy stand in montauk went missing i knew
to dig the earth, to steal a lock of your hair,
to play 90s commercials backwards, it wasn't about
getting you back. no, silly. it was time travel.
my rhinestones, my purple, my necklace that couldn't
be traded like love or baseball cards. i raised the dead
to smell a fountain soda that still tastes like sunscreen and

curiosity. i always had the sight. the sight is better than any rerun.

friend request

💀 💀 💀 💀 💀 💀 💀 💀

💀 💀 we had sex once. 💀 💀

💀 💀 it was exactly fine. 💀 💀

💀 💀 💀 💀 💀 💀 💀 💀

sex psychic

first things first hot shot, i am so good
at being lonely, i'm always the little spoon,
maraschino cherries top off any dessert,
i'll always triple text you,
especially if we're a throuple, and no,
i'll never care about looking eager, in my
town, beauty never runs dry. why should it?
i know what you like, because you always
like what you like, like vanilla ice cream in
a heat wave, like cactus and avocado tacos,
you're predictable but maybe off-beat, i know
you'll never forget me, not me, sugar & spice,
everything nice, like a cutie pie, a flame,
my chocolate cherry head in between your thighs.

midnight tigers

yellow, at dawn
we realized *The Craft* has
                    n o t h i n g

                                on us

just corn syrup, fake wounds
glare in alchemy,
rags filled with rhinestones

false diamonds
cast no spell, but i l l u s i o n
snared, wretched
forest palm leaves,

impulse cloistered
for teenage boys, true,
all the girls
we kissed in bathrooms,

like wine and honey,
grave, and motion
is a blow job
in a jeep grand cherokee
in rage, like

                    c h a r r i n g

the sun rises,
burns, beauty rage

furnace-fear, mirrors,
alchemy, a rite of woe
remember our teeth,
how sharp,
delicious is the meat.

peace offering

i expect men to tell me i'm pretty

it's the least they can do.

solar eclipse in pisces

pisces, you are the sacred harmony of fantasy and reality. you are a poet's poet — dreamy, contemplative, ethereal, and emotionally intuitive. you converse with warmth and come across with emotional integrity to a fault. as you move through the world and the cosmos with reverence for all things tangible and dream-based, you adapt well. you apply empathy to all energies, big and small. this might strike as being indecisive, but it's really using both earthly and metaphysical tools at your disposal to lean into sensuality and purpose.

direct message

i'm not calm, i'm experiencing a cardiac event
rereading messages without responding is a form of self-care.

sugar baby

i am not as interesting as i think i am. this is a story about mirrors.

i email heaven's gate like i am shaking a magic 8-ball.
the answer is yes and we email every other day. tuesdays are the
best.

i email them before dates, long hours before i check my phone
for any response.

i am afraid of a cult ghosting me.
i am ghosting myself, and my past. i email heaven's gate instead.

do you miss your friends?
we miss their vehicles, they'll be back someday

i kissed a stranger after three $15 cocktails
i never pay for them, i never even make a move to grab my wallet.
i palm $100 bills into my purse like it's nothing.

are you waiting for a trail of stardust to pick you up?
can't say so now

sometimes my $15 cocktails are $20 cocktails. two martinis in, i talk
about comets.
there's a nebula in my throat and i hold my breath when i pass a
mirror.
i hold my breath because it's a wish.

free yourself from love. everything regenerates.

everything returns. you'll see.

mystique

i had an emotional affair
with a married man,
i wasn't married
so who cares?

vows are vows are vows
are promises,
that should be kept
but not always

i had an emotional affair
with text messages,
we never met

just swiped
sexted
and sexted
he told me
i was

some
sacred
holy
enchanting
beautiful
thing

texting turned
into imessages
good mornings
good nights
i called him

in ubers home
from dates
with men
from dates with couples
that i didn't let fuck me

you sound like
velvet syrup,
he said

i let myself
melt into a puddle
pretending to be
someone else

i sexted him:
my favorite x-men
is
mystique

she is blue
and beautiful
and you hardly see her
because she is
always someone else

is it a personal gain?
a fetish?
a fascination?

the married man
says i am better
than anything
he's read before

i am multitudes,
so he says,
because i am beauty
and comic books

women are deeper
than that, i say

mystique has
all of the power
the x-men don't
give her enough credit

i wonder what his skin tastes like
will i know? probably not
mystique doesn't need taste
just imagining

i don't need
to know him
to be intoxicated
the allure is
his phone ringing me
a text message left hanging
the real allure is
he is a box
a string of numbers
that wants me
wants to do
whatever he wants to me
delicious, juicy
i am on drugs
without drugs
that is mystique,

that is wanting.

the married man says,
my wife knows about you
she doesn't care,
neither do i.

neptune in the 8th house

suggests a mystical sort of person,
a person obsessed with love, sex, and death.

i'm a hybrid model,
not interested in the material world.

i'm an oracle of delphi: put yourself
inside my pussy, the vessel.

lana gave me my money anthem,

we'll die a thousand deaths.

the actor

the actor showed up on your feed one day, you didn't know each
other
but then you did,
you became a tiny photo with red lips, an enthusiastic text box, a
fembot,
as heart eyes, likes, exclamation points
you read his status updates in that TV cop voice,
then you read his messages to you,
as that spoiled financier brother having an affair:
you marvelous poet
you remarkable leonine woman
talking to you is a blessing,
this day is a blessing,
our connection is a blessing,
he starts texting you while you're on a bad tinder date
bubble-head, this isn't your first telephone romance rodeo
he tells you to call him sometime
he doesn't want to sit in front of the computer or a phone screen
the actor says: i want to hear your voice
the actor drops his phone number
as if you never thought about fucking him when you were fifteen
the actor thinks it's sweet that you both grew up in New York
you are both suburban kids who couldn't wait to get out
the actor always calls first, you never get to pull the trigger
his voice so familiar, the voice from your TV,
this time this voice is all for you
the actor asks you questions, the actor interviews
the actor listens intently
the actor is so New York but so Los Angeles
the actor says he can tell you both have a spiritual connection
the actor wishes you a happy birthday, your birthdays are five days
apart
the actor is unfiltered, the actor isn't flustered by your past or

present
after all, he's an ethical non-monogamist
the actor doesn't bat an eye when you whimper about getting
dumped
by a man and a woman and you loved them both so much
instead, the actor wants to know more
how you three held hands in public, how you kissed,
he always gets stuck on the kissing, but the actor never asks about
the sex
he didn't ask how three people fuck and sweat and cum at the same
time
even though you wanted him to know you were in the middle
the actor is still a gentleman
the actor breathes into the phone, you want him to breathe into your
neck
the actor says yoga brought him to a higher plane
the actor lives in west hollywood
the actor is impressed that you almost moved to LA twice
the actor says you are a very New York girl
but, the actor understands how you could try to exist in LA and New
York
the actor says there is grit in your spirit
the actor wants to call you after his boxing class
at 1am, he emails you a treatment for a TV show with one question:
what do you think? I trust you
the actor reads all of your poems on the internet and you never
asked him to
at 2:37 am, you sent the actor a short story about a love affair with
Frank Sinatra
really, you took all of the older men you loved and tried to love
and fit them into seven neat pages
and in this story Frank calls his side chick *young lady*
the actor asks what you're wearing
the actor says he called women he is close with spirit-sisters
the actor says your voice is a blessing

you would twist your voice around the air waves if you could

the actor says it's time to share Google calendars and meet

the actor is gruff and asks you about LA

the actor wants to show you Laurel Canyon

the actor has been in love but doesn't talk about it

the actor only calls, never texts

the actor has given some thought to fucking you,

your wet thighs in the kitchen

the actor speaks slowly

the actor is ethical

the actor calls you young lady at the end of a phone call

the actor disappears

the actor reappears and says *happy birthday, baby*

you find the actor's brother on tinder but swipe left

the actor asks how the summer is treating you

the actor wants you to know how nice LA is this time of year

the actor says you are long overdue for a present

he would like to take you to a yoga class,

and out for dinner. it's his treat.

push notification

honestly,
i wanted
you

aching,
for ages,

like sour
cherries

plump,
pleasant,
mis-
leading

i don't
know
what to do

once
i get you.

tarot talks back

the major arcana never lies
and it's telling me not to be such a little bitch.

one day i'll be the maiden-mother-crone,
some kind of witch with some kind of magick.

right now, i feel empty like a piece
of sea glass waiting to be picked.

i wish i was a vampire, but i'll never
be that interesting.

to be something enchanted would be
so dark and delightful, don't you think?

.

moonlight

the first time i read a tarot card,
it was like having sex, or turning into a real marilyn

maybe it was the sadness, maybe it was having a crush on a girl
it was having a crush on a girl who had the name moonlight,

it was having a crush who never knew i had the crush,
my crush was very marilyn, dreamy, wanton, moody blue

my college feral lips pulled at cards, so what if i had a boyfriend
marilyn had boyfriends, maybe girlfriends too,
like marilyn, i could be a siren, calling sirens, my hair
moonlight girl's hair crashing against rocks, we beauty queens

long lashes, coney island ice cream screaming, just us girls
in my marilyn dreams, we were all long legs in short-shorts

with three cards, i was syrup all over, an alchemist's voice
thick, needling, in power

i felt like tight muscles quivering all over: moonlight's eyes
all on me, all on me, was i pretty? was i power?

maybe it was both. moonlight wait, but like marilyn,
it feels dark. speak, moonlight says.

i see, i almost come: a change, a warrior's bow.

a boyfriend break up. she didn't call for me again.

after a glass or two, i am ready to confess. my fetish is spilling it all on a first date. when grainy photos were a thing, i figured out how to see web cam girls without paying for it. i wanted to be them. i wanted to kiss them. it was hard for me to conceptualize actually having sex or wanting to have sex. i knew i wanted to have sex at some point or another. i knew i wanted to have sex at some point or another before i was 18 or 21. i didn't really worry about it. it would happen sooner or later. but i fell in love with these women. feminine and powerful and they hunted. they were hungry. they knew what they wanted. they were equal parts self aware and unaware. i remember finding their profiles on social sites before social networking was a thing. i read their blogs. i read their thoughts. the tv shows they liked. the kind of take out they ordered. the politically uncorrect thoughts they had. the curves they were ahead of. music playlists they made and streamed before streaming made sense. i knew their real names. their problems. i still wanted to taste their lipstick to feel them and feel myself. i still don't want to fuck them, now as an adult with my own lipstick, my own hips, my own femme-ness that means nothing and everything. i still wonder what they look like in front of their computers. their computers are laptops now. some of them are married. i wonder if they are happy. if they take selfies and wonder is this all there is. i'm glad it's all there is.

i don't know
if i want to

believe in gods
or a god

i'll pray at
your feet

please make
everything feel
opalescent

now and
forever
and i'll

pray
and you,
you can

run your tongue
over my teeth

again and
again.

procrastination fantasy

it's cliché but i always wanted to fuck a surfer,

disinterested sunscreen and scented shell necklaces.

i miss live journal

i miss the wonder of an empty text box

i miss my scratched pink razr
with limited text messages
a paltry offering of three saved texts

name
password
press enter

writing a post,
i miss holding
a shitty megapixel camera
earnestly trying

for a pretty photo

my voice
in a square shape
talking to an empty room

the blue screen
colored my face

a witty username
a grainy 100 x 100 pixel icon
use would still say
what pretty lips i have
& my, how thick they are

made the click-clack
with my keys
& swooned over pictures

on shitty dial up
that we all shared

the room would talk back
& the room knew how i felt

when a softer world was new
every sunday
with make out clubs
& sad, big eyed boys
on their static, muffled guitars

that always threatened to get louder
like hungry wolf fingers

typing,
clambering for answers
among tarot cards
with mouths full
of saliva & blood

i miss live journal
i miss calling out my song
finding a new voice
threaded in the keys

calling out to an empty room
& waiting for the room
to answer back.

falling in love

responsibility is like having sex: i want all of it or none of it. i don't
know what dying feels like, but i'm good at imagining. if grades
were given out for daydreaming, i would be the valedictorian, or
an olympic gold medalist. whichever one is sexier. feelings are a
construct or a method of survival. it depends on what emotion you
need for a dopamine hit or to stop breathing. i can remember long
walks on the beach but i can't tell you anyone's cell phone number.
breathing is blurry, but i assume it's this way for everyone. do you
like my smile? i want to be your lover if you'd only ask me to be
your internet girlfriend. i am more interested in chatting with you
online and basking in our collaborative fantasies. so when i send
you an email every day, it's because i'm delighting in a panic attack
imagining you reading my words. the best feeling is a bold subject
line in my inbox. dying young is an art for fools. every morning i pray
at the holy trinity of menthol cigarettes, phone scrolling, and black
coffee. what i'm trying to ask you is what does this feel like?

left on read

♥ ♥ ♥ ♥ ♥ ♥ ♥ ♥ ♥ ♥ ♥
♥ ♥ ♥ ♥ ♥ ♥ ♥ ♥ ♥ ♥ ♥
♥ ♥ ♥ make me howl ♥ ♥ ♥
♥ ♥ ♥ ♥ ♥ ♥ ♥ ♥ ♥ ♥ ♥
♥ ♥ like a spoiled brat ♥ ♥
♥ ♥ ♥ ♥ ♥ ♥ ♥ ♥ ♥ ♥ ♥
♥ ♥ ♥ ♥ ♥ ♥ ♥ ♥ ♥ ♥ ♥

portrait as a chatbot

1. does this dress come in black?
2. i am thinking about coffee.
3. i don't smoke, but who has a cigarette?
4. my dream is to be surrounded by puppies.
5. everyone is so dumb.
6. why though?
7. pizza tonight?
8. thanks! I bought it for $10.
9. i mean, don't you agree?
10. i need to exit this planet immediately.

i've been to bigger forests with even
bigger secrets

it's true what they say: the forest keeps the secrets of the universe
of course, i can't say where or how, that would be breaking a
contract
there's a website that will tell you how to get there.

darling, i signed my name away long ago. we all did.
you didn't get the paperwork yet. it's full of dark howls and
overnight shipping.
it's full of jewels and songs. it's full of night in its endless pearls.

i hope, when you get to the end, you don't miss the last clause.
darling, it's important. read harder. the real joke is: we are the
ghosts.

stop hiding. you're only hiding from yourself.

>cast a spell on 56k dialup

>start>open program
>real ruby blues
>>dynamite diamonds
>>>pathway clear>enter

>i kissed more girls than boys their hips
>>are beautiful
>i want to wear iridescent wings
>>and burn wood>be free

>daydreaming is more than sport
>i'm in love with an aim message
>no, really
>>love it text and emoticons

>>am i the computer or is the computer me?

>are all humans like this?
>soft, blue-purple veins under skin?

>scamming up ways to never work

>i'm human but i'm not sure what that feels like
>if i wrote my own program i'd change the ending
>a woman in glasses spells revenge
>>i want revenge in red lipstick

>if i'm hurt
>i envision black water spilling

>out of your mouth

>it's endless

>the program overrides
>unable to load>illegal operation
>lung capacity depleted
>>dull rubies
>>>all web cams are witches>screenshot me

>no one is supposed to be here
>log out>forget

magic 8-ball

as i see it, yes
wishes part clearly
the sun shines on olive trees

ask again later
write the rules of the game
then change the rules of the game

better not tell you now
cannot predict now

divination is my biggest
achilles heel
i am the past
present and future

concentrate and ask again
don't count on it

my dreams whisper in the dark

it is certain
i shake in honey clover dew
i dream
somewhere, you dream

it is decidedly so
most likely
i live
and forget

my reply is no
my sources say no
outlook not so good

reply hazy try again
signs point to yes
very doubtful

worries are worthless
anxiety is just free rent
i never think that i hold
all of the cards in the deck
answers flow like olives and oil
i'm not an oracle where
all of the gods say yes
use the internet
instead

outlook good
petalvoiced, bittersweet
i want to love you
when i know you
pour honey on me, honey
if only life could be
this simple.

without a doubt
yes
yes, definitely
you may rely on it.

final_version.jpg

in this rented universe, everything is ethereal
spinning holographic glitter, dizzying rhinestones
with a libra's strength, we trade secrets:
gold, women warriors, foxes, blood from wine.

the myth is, you and i tell each other we are
precious, rare creatures, we are beholden
but we are scarred, i only have one gift:
surviving a horror movie with my song

you are grace, and most gems: a ram, rational
you asked death if it was real once, and yet
both of you prevailed. i don't know if that's winning.

my sacred horse, i can tell you it's not losing.

oracles

here is how our great romance ends:
i'll never say hello to you in an empty bar,
i'll sell your tee shirt, but keep the sweatshirt
i'll read all of your social media for subtweets,
i'll meditate in the mornings on forgiveness,
i'll delete all of your emails unread, a purge without a great fire,
i'll walk the dog holding a joint, holding keys in between
my knuckles as if i'm persephone holding

pomegranate seeds over your throat.

my dead boyfriend still follows me on instagram

i wasn't expecting you.
truthfully, almost forgotten
you turned up in heart-shapes
late at night, always after 3 am
you like my photos, you leave
unicorn emojis, but you don't speak
i wasn't concerned until you slid
into my DMs.

if these divination tools could talk

i am more than an oracle. these surfaces hold voices in a land beyond milk and honey.

if you knew me, intimately, like a dinner party guest, you'd know i am more than this.

your mother comes through. why? aunts and grandmothers like shanties or choruses.

really, it's the little grey cat you petted once on a walk home from school.

that's who is waiting on the line. it's my favorite caller.

a phone operator. a wire service for the dead. don't ask for dead presidents.

they were never great conversationalists without speech writers.

poets, always a good choice. they'll never hang up the line.

if it's out of network, move the planchette or pendulum again.

why haven't you considered calling in the woods, near a water source?

the connection is hydrated. it's good for your skin.

basement readings with wall-to-wall carpeting is the lowest form of communication.

no, i don't know why your dearly departed said *glass marbles*, *rum*, and *worry,* either.

if you think it's a demon, it's probably a demon.

if you think the ghost is in love with you, it's a demon.

dogs don't get enough pets. i said what i said.

i let you think you're a psychic. just like you think he's going to text you back.

your living room has dead zones with speckled static.

the color scheme is terrible by the way.

personal comfort

jubilee, memory is a ghost. let me explain.

in the morning, a man i pretended to love, said: *you were a mistake*.

like he discovered the arch of the covenant, or buried treasure in the wall.

he storms in on you in the shower — hot, steamy, pulls back the curtain. there is no sound. just white noise. it would be a hot porno, except it's not.

i cower. i never come. i don't know which happened first: the sneering, or the blood. everytime i have sex with him, i disassociate and think of fucking someone else. someone beautiful and kind with warm hands. someone with an archangel's nose and a better voice.

a broken record that sounds like yellow wallpaper stains my thoughts. this is how ghost stories begin.

there is a new mirror. there are new records. flash forward.

thunderstorms in summer — a marble angel holds my hand. there is the moon. there are no church bells at night.

in my dream, i float. in my dream, i kiss my girlfriend all over her mouth. blood runs down our lips. this love is never for you.

forever sext

i like making out with you because you remind me of the internet.

i like making out with you because you make me feel attractive.

around you, age doesn't seem to exist. my body doesn't seem to exist.

i am floating. i am a beam of light. i am an angel on a cloud.

around you, i drink. i am both things i love and hate: rush and addiction.

when i get a buzz, i want to confess. i want you to think my secrets are sexy.

are my secrets sexy? my secrets are translucents mirrors.

my secrets have secrets of their own. my secrets crushes on girls.

my secret is that i want to look like me: red lips, rosary necklace, tight skirt.

my secret is that i want to look like this and i want you to call me your boyfriend.

my secret is banal, my secret is every secret.

my secret is a prayer and i kiss your mouth with it.

i'm an adult now. but i'm a girl in your arms. i'm a boyfriend when i need to be.

i'm an adult, but everything i needed to learn i learned from gurlpages.

if we met and fell in love earlier, we'd take shitty flip phone photos together.

i'd post the photos everywhere. maybe i'd finally come out.

my secret is i love drunk texting you.

my thighs are wet. i miss your lips. i have a body again. i have big tits.

my secret is i love when you respond. my secret is i love when you egg me on.

my lips are bee stings. i'm pulsating. my body is a wolf. my body is a ghost.

my secret is that i fell in love with you and out of love with you at the same time.

my secret is i can't stop sexting you. forever sext. forever reply back.

are you there? let's time travel and start a webring and own the internet.

are you there? i'm your internet girlfriend.

```
program installation
```

mod x+x *internet_girlfriend.bin*

welcome to your setup wizard,
few things in life feel as good as botox.

it is strongly recommended that you exit all programs,
before engaging in any lip fillers or treatments.

love is someone who calls me witchy spice,
the true bisexual narrative expansion pack is loading.

click next, and i'll turn you into an owl,
just for an evening or two. until you love me.

cold coffee is the best tincture for regret
in my case, breakfast.

do you know i am a witch?
i am a rising moon full of snakes.

do you want to save or run this file?

PATH=$GRLFRND_HOME/bin:$PATH; export PATH

my life with the cult

shitty webcam, cat ears headband, uninterrupted net.
i'm a cat girl today, brown hair turned red, premium fantasy.

my vices include holding my breath when passing a cemetery
doom scrolling endlessly on reddit and making eye contact with
myself in the cam.

sign on to chat, put me in the center of your cyber fantasies.
i'm a good slut, i'm the best slut. love me like you own me.

call me mommy call me daddy call me sweet thing.
call me by any name. call me a name. names are irrelevant.

what's your name angel? *i don't have a name.*

`the_truth.exe`

what i'm really saying:

        pleasure is all i want from you

        glue crystal teardrop-shaped rhinestones to

        my face and fuck me like a saint in ecstasy.

we avoid facing reality.

        deal with jupiter and then get back to me

        intense and deep is the cusp of this house.

be a sweet death

        esoteric, spiritual, and mysterious
        complex possessions and sacrifices

        ancient deities with seahorses and freshwater

bookmark me like one of your favorite websites

        is it naive to love you?

        then, let me be naive on a fool's journey.

it can be hard to integrate within this planet.

it happened to me: i kissed a gravedigger

we met on on okcupid
i didn't know your
type of living

i was 25
& absent-minded

in truth,
you bored me

then, i heard
you made space
for the dead

i knew, i had to
for prosperity
for thrashing
for screaming
into grey moonlight

because liking slayer
& ripped tee shirts at 19
wasn't enough

sorry, darling
i need street cred

my lips went ghostly
overripe & purple veined

in my dreams that night,
i pulled pulpy petals
out of my teeth

the next day,
i had to wear dark lipstick
to hide teeth marks
in little bloated shapes

girls at the office
asked if i got juvederm
i didn't say no.

things men from the internet say to me on dates

you're so young.
i'm so glad you're not dead.
can we split this?
we should climb a mountain.
i'm neurotic, i want to know what you think.
how would you feel about becoming the governor's wife?
well, in a few years, you might be incapacitated. with babies.
i never told anyone this before. not even my ex-wife.
i want to give you ten thousand dollars. i want you to be happy.
let's get married. right now.
i'm a feminist. you didn't think i would pay for dinner, did you?
we would be great at being rich. spend it all on spas and shit.
i think...the sluttier, the better.
sorry i flaked out. i had a kitten emergency.
i just want to date your hair.
stay with me.
it's official: you are a fox.

palmistry

in the future, you will swipe on romantic prospects like discount bin *guess who?* cards

in the future, you won't admit that you still use a magic 8-ball

in the future, you will inject poison into your face and you'll savor the feeling of muscles seizing

in the future, you will enjoy waking up early

in the future, you'll break up with someone because they read the wrong books

in the future, you'll break up with someone because they don't read any books

in the future, you have a one-thousand dollar phone, so will everyone else

in the future, you realize that Sporty Spice is the only Spice Girl worth being

in the future, you'll have one broken engagement and you'll thank god for it
in the future, you'll sit on a beach and realize the world isn't *boy talk* or *mall madness*

in the future, you're lucky to be alive

in the future, you're someone's sugar baby for 120 days

in the future, you consider being a phone sex operator

in the future, you don't because you'll have to buy a landline

in the future, you don't because that also means you'll have to talk to people

in the future, you wonder how anyone gets by without a dog

in the future, you wonder if this is all there is

in the future, you snort cocaine in a dive bar bathroom next to a roach in the future, you don't run out of the bathroom

in the future, you'll muster up the courage to hold a woman's hand
in public

in the future, you'll be crushed when she ghosts you
in the future, you'll laugh at men and worry about getting killed

in the future, you think about jumping out of a window too often

in the future, you think about throwing your phone out of a window
for no reason

in the future, it bothers you more and more

in the future, you'll learn to love yourself and it feels strange

acknowledgements

for you :)

thank you to leza, christoph, and lindsay lehrman for believing in my work. thank you to joanna, for your endless support and editing prowess. thank you to tom and pepper.

+ adventures in the makeup club contains partial and full found phrases from MOC profiles that I wrote down in a notebook as a teen.

+ blue rosaries was published in Catland's Venefica.

+ cult classic and portrait of a vsco girl was published in Be About It Zine

+ final_version.jpg was published in Pussy Magic

+ i miss live journal was published in Internet Friends

+ internet girlfriend was published in Hobart

+ i've been to bigger forests with even bigger secrets was published in The Mantle

+ midnight tigers contains an aubade with thanks to Philip Larkin and John Donne

+ night time ice cream was published in Pine Hills Review

+ pink plastic caboodle was publish in Plainsongs

+ portrait of a vsco girl borrows lines from the Rolling Stones, Britney Spears, and the Velvet Underground

+ relax, kristy it's just the dark lord was published in Black Telephone Magazine

+ my dead boyfriend still follows me on instagram, you vs. the girl they told you not to worry about, and you'd think i was a witch or somethin' was published in Heroin Chic.

+ the_truth.exe contains found and reworked phrases with thanks from advanced astrology and dream astro meanings.

Stephanie Valente

Stephanie Valente is a poet and a witch in New York. This is her debut full-length collection. Other published chapbooks include Hotel Ghost, waiting for the end of the world, Little Fang, and Spell Work (Bottlecap Press & Giallo). Her work has appeared in Witch Craft Magazine, Maudlin House, and Hobart. She is the associate editor at Yes, Poetry. stephanievalente.com

Also by Clash Books

GAG REFLEX
Elle Nash

WHAT ARE YOU
Lindsay Lerman

PSYCHROS
Charlene Elsby

AT SEA
Aïcha Martine Thiam

THE SMALLEST OF BONES
Holly Lyn Walrath

AN EXHALATION OF DEAD THINGS
Savannah Slone

WATERFALL GIRLS
Kimberly White

ALL THE PLACES I WISH I DIED
Crystal Stone

LIFE OF THE PARTY
Tea-Hacic-Vlahovic

GIRL LIKE A BOMB
Autumn Christian

THE ELVIS MACHINE
Kim Vodicka

WE PUT THE LIT IN LITERARY

clashbooks.com

 @clashbooks  @clashbooks /clashbooks

Email
clashmediabooks@gmail.com